DISCOVERING THE UNITED STATES

South Carolina

BY DAVID J. CLARKE

An Imprint of Abdo Publishing
abdobooks.com

abdobooks.com

Printed in China.
052024
092024

Cover Photo: Sean Pavone/Shutterstock Images
Interior Photos: Vive Media/Shutterstock Images, 4–5, 28 (top right); Bonnie Taylor Barry/Shutterstock Images, 7 (top left); Bob Hendry/Shutterstock Images, 7 (top right); Alina M. Darkhovsky/Shutterstock Images, 7 (bottom left); Tory Kallman/Shutterstock Images, 7 (bottom right); Shutterstock Images, 9, 18, 28 (bottom left); Prentiss Findlay/Shutterstock Images, 10; Print Collector/Hulton Archive/Getty Images, 12–13; Marvel Studios/Walt Disney Pictures/Album/Alamy, 15; James Kirkikis/Shutterstock Images, 16; Kevin Ruck/Shutterstock Images, 20–21; Jonathan A. Mauer/Shutterstock Images, 22; Chris Carlson/AP Images, 25; Sean Pavone/Shutterstock Images, 26; Red Line Editorial, 28 (top left), 29; Grindstone Media Group/Shutterstock Images, 28 (bottom right)

Editor: Marley Richmond
Series Designer: Katharine Hale

Library of Congress Control Number: 2023949369

Publisher's Cataloging-in-Publication Data

Names: Clarke, David J., author.
Title: South Carolina / by David J. Clarke
Description: Minneapolis, Minnesota: Abdo Publishing, 2025 | Series: Discovering the United States | Includes online resources and index.
Identifiers: ISBN 9781098294113 (lib. bdg.) | ISBN 9798384913382 (ebook)
Subjects: LCSH: U.S. states--Juvenile literature. | South Carolina--History--Juvenile literature. | Southeastern States--Juvenile literature. | Physical geography--United States--Juvenile literature.
Classification: DDC 973--dc23

All population data taken from:
"Estimates of Population by Sex, Race, and Hispanic Origin: April 1, 2020 to July 1, 2022." *US Census Bureau, Population Division*, June 2023, census.gov.

CONTENTS

The Arthur Ravenel Jr. Bridge needed to be tall enough for ships to sail underneath it. The main bridge is almost 200 feet (61 m) above the water.

CHAPTER 1

The Diamond Bridge

On July 9, 2005, a huge crowd gathered in Charleston, South Carolina. The people walked 2.5 miles (4 km) across the new Arthur Ravenel Jr. Bridge. The walk kicked off a week-long celebration that included a ceremony and fireworks.

The new bridge crosses the Cooper River. It replaced two older bridges that were no longer safe. The Ravenel Bridge features two towers shaped like diamonds. The shape is made from cable **stays**, which hold up the bridge. It is the longest cable-stayed bridge in North America. The bridge is considered one of Charleston's most beautiful features.

Hurricane Proof

The Ravenel Bridge was made to stay strong even in violent weather. It can withstand winds up to 300 miles per hour (480 km/h). That is strong enough to make it through even the worst hurricanes.

South Carolina Facts

DATE OF STATEHOOD
May 23, 1788

CAPITAL
Columbia

POPULATION
5,282,634

AREA
32,020 square miles
(82,931 sq km)

STATE BIRD

Carolina wren

STATE TREE

Palmetto

STATE FLOWER

Yellow jessamine

STATE MARINE MAMMAL

Bottlenose dolphin

Each US state has a different population, size, and capital city. States also have state symbols.

South Carolina's Land

South Carolina is in the South region of the United States. North Carolina lies to the north.

Georgia is to the south and west. The Savannah River runs along this border. South Carolina's eastern border is along the Atlantic Ocean.

The Blue Ridge Mountains run through northwestern South Carolina. The central and eastern parts of the state are very flat. The eastern part of South Carolina is called the Coastal Plain. This part of the state is very close to sea level. Because of this, the area is often called the Lowcountry.

South Carolina is known for its thick forests. The state is covered in tall loblolly pine trees. In the east, there are many types of trees, including magnolias, live oaks, and cypresses. These trees are often covered with a thin white plant called Spanish moss.

Spanish moss grows in places that are warm and wet. It is common near South Carolina's coasts.

South Carolina's two largest lakes are in the south-central part of the state. They are called Lake Marion and Lake Moultrie. The lakes are connected by the Diversion Canal. The Pee Dee River and Savannah River are the two longest rivers in South Carolina.

Hurricanes can bring high winds, heavy rainfall, and large waves to South Carolina.

South Carolina's Climate

South Carolina has four seasons. Winters are very short and mild. It rarely snows in the state.

Summers are hot and humid. Spring and fall are warm.

Some tornadoes come in the spring. Hurricanes can hit South Carolina in summer and fall. This time of year is known as hurricane season. The state also gets ten to 15 earthquakes every year. But most of them are not very powerful.

Further Evidence

Look at the website below. Does it give any new evidence to support Chapter One?

South Carolina

abdocorelibrary.com/discovering-south-carolina

Sir Alexander Cuming, *left*, was a British explorer who traveled to South Carolina in 1729. The British king sent Cuming to meet with the Cherokee people.

CHAPTER 2

The People of South Carolina

The first people in South Carolina were American Indians. They arrived in the region about 13,000 years ago. Nearly 30 nations called South Carolina home. The largest nations were the Catawba and the Cherokee. These nations still exist today.

European **settlers** began arriving in the 1500s. By 1840, Europeans had forced most American Indians in South Carolina to leave their land.

In the late 1600s, English settlers began bringing **enslaved** Africans to South Carolina. Many enslaved people arrived through Charleston. They were then forced to work on farms and **plantations**. Slavery was outlawed in the United States in the 1860s.

Today the population of South Carolina is about 64 percent white. Another 26 percent is Black. About 7 percent is Hispanic or Latino, and 2 percent is Asian. Less than 1 percent is American Indian.

Some famous people come from South Carolina. Actor Chadwick Boseman

Chadwick Boseman acted in many popular movies. One of his most famous parts was playing T'Challa in the movie *Black Panther*.

was born there. So was the soul musician James Brown.

Culture

Some people in coastal areas of South Carolina speak a language called Gullah, or Gullah Geechee. Many enslaved people spoke different West African languages. Gullah is a combination of these languages and English. The culture is still celebrated today.

Many Gullah people make baskets out of sweetgrass.

Gullah people make unique food, music, and art. Basket weaving is one part of Gullah culture.

College sports are a big part of South Carolina's culture. The state's two biggest colleges are the University of South Carolina and Clemson University. Their **annual** football game is called the Palmetto Bowl. The University of South Carolina women's basketball team is also one of the best in the country.

Industry

Many South Carolinians work in the shipping industry. The Charleston **port** is one of the busiest in North America. Each day, large **cargo** ships enter and exit the port with goods going to and coming from places all over the world.

Darlington Raceway

Darlington Raceway is in the northern part of South Carolina. It hosts NASCAR races every year. Darlington has a fast track and very difficult corners. Some fans call it The Track Too Tough to Tame.

South Carolina's flag shows a palmetto tree. This is because logs from Palmetto trees were used to make a shelter during the Revolutionary War (1775–1783).

The auto industry is also important in South Carolina. Michelin makes many of its tires at a plant in Greenville. The ZF Group is based in Gray Court. This company develops technology designed to make cars safer.

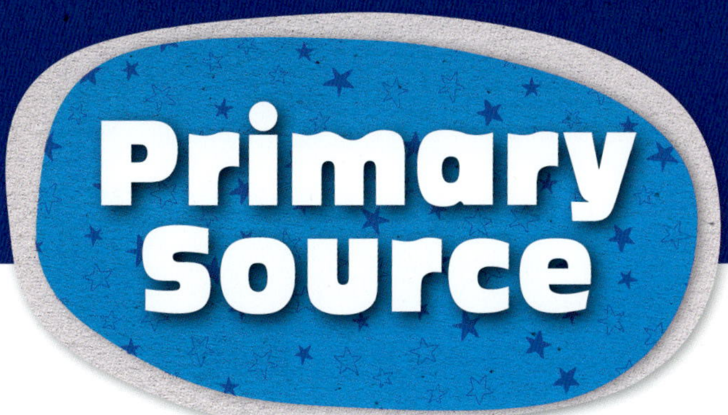

Michael Smalls comes from a family that has been making Gullah baskets for generations. He spoke about the proud tradition:

> Our ancestors were able to create such beautiful things, even in the harshness of how they were treated on the plantations. . . . They were still able to continue their culture.

Source: Kenneth Moton, Janice McDonald, and Kimberly Ruiz. "Preserving the Gullah Geechee Culture in the US." *ABC News*, 1 Mar. 2022, abcnews.go.com. Accessed 14 Nov. 2023.

What's the Big Idea?

Read this quote carefully. What is its main idea? Explain how the main idea is supported by details.

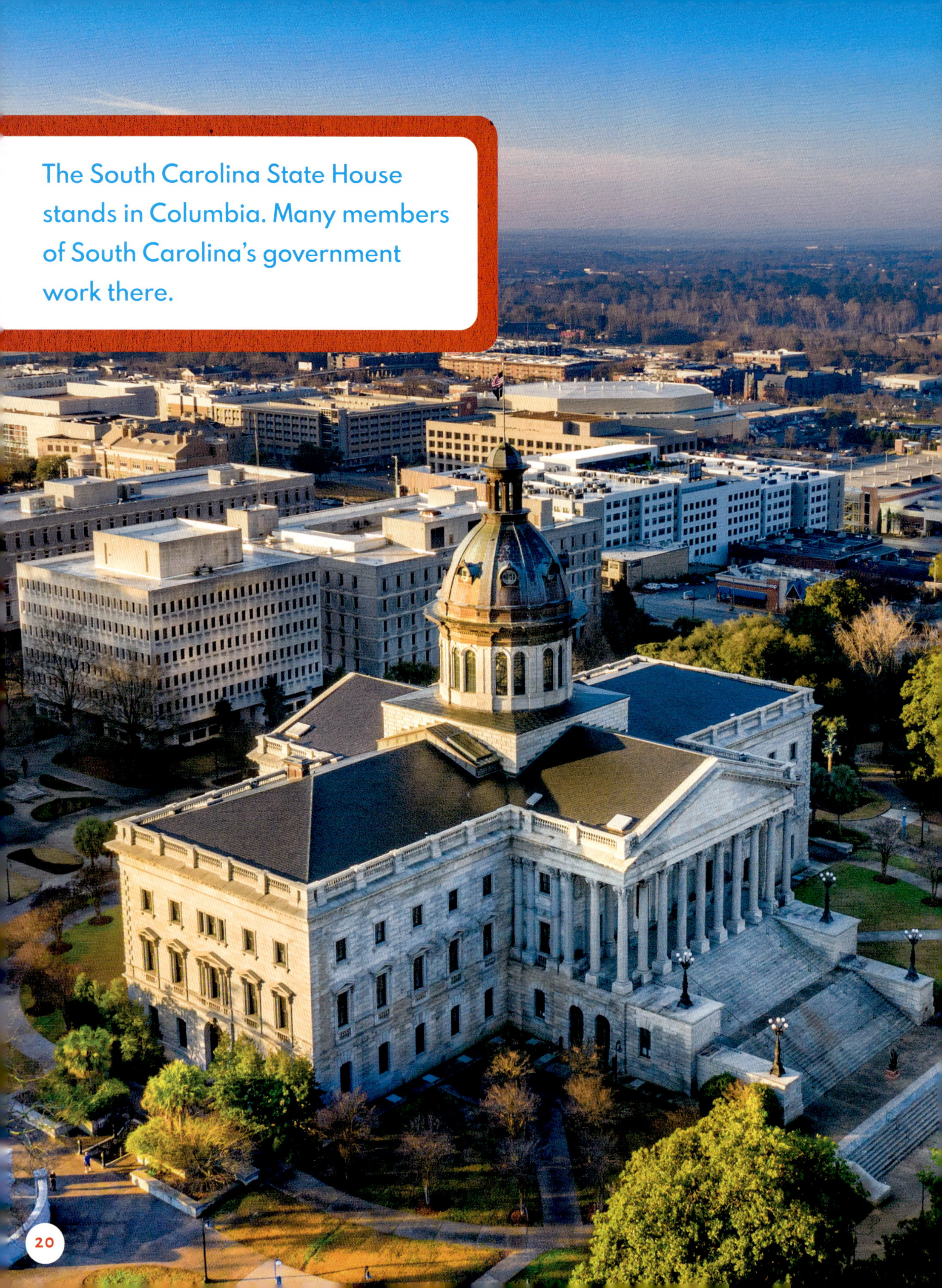

The South Carolina State House stands in Columbia. Many members of South Carolina's government work there.

CHAPTER 3

Places in South Carolina

South Carolina's capital is Columbia. The city is also home to the University of South Carolina. The largest city in the state is Charleston. Other large cities include Greenville and Myrtle Beach.

The boardwalk trail takes visitors through Congaree National Park.

Parks

South Carolina's only national park is Congaree National Park. It is known for its trees, including the loblolly pine. The forest canopy at Congaree is one of the tallest in the eastern United States.

In Woods Bay State Park, visitors can see pools of fresh water shaped like eggs. These are called Carolina Bays. No one knows exactly how they formed.

In the northwest corner of South Carolina is Headwaters State Forest. It is home to Sassafras Mountain. This is the tallest mountain in the state. Sassafras Mountain is on the border of North and South Carolina. On the mountain, it is possible to stand in both states at the same time.

Landmarks

Fort Sumter National Monument sits on an island in Charleston Harbor. The American Civil War (1861–1865) began when Southern soldiers bombed Northern soldiers inside the fort. The battle started on April 12, 1861.

The International African American Museum is also in Charleston. The museum shows the journeys and struggles of Black Americans

The Holy City

Charleston's nickname is the Holy City. Today Charleston has more than 400 churches and other religious buildings. They represent different faiths. The oldest church is Saint Andrew's Parish Church. It was built in 1706.

The International African American Museum opened in 2023. Tonya Matthews, the museum's president, poses in front of an exhibit at the opening.

through art and historical exhibits. It sits on Gadsden's Wharf. That was the site where many African people were sold into slavery.

More than 17 million people visit Myrtle Beach every year.

The Grand Strand is north of Charleston. It is a 60-mile (97-km) beach. Part of the beach includes the Myrtle Beach Boardwalk and Promenade. Visitors there can fish on the pier and ride the SkyWheel. This Ferris wheel is 187 feet (60 m) tall.

South Carolina is full of history and natural beauty. Museums and monuments teach visitors about the people who have called the state home. Visitors can enjoy South Carolina's beaches and parks or cheer on sports teams. There is something for everyone in the state.

Explore Online

Visit the website below. What new information did you learn about the International African American Museum that wasn't in Chapter Three?

International African American Museum

abdocorelibrary.com/discovering-south-carolina

State Map

KEY

Capital

Park

City or town

Point of interest

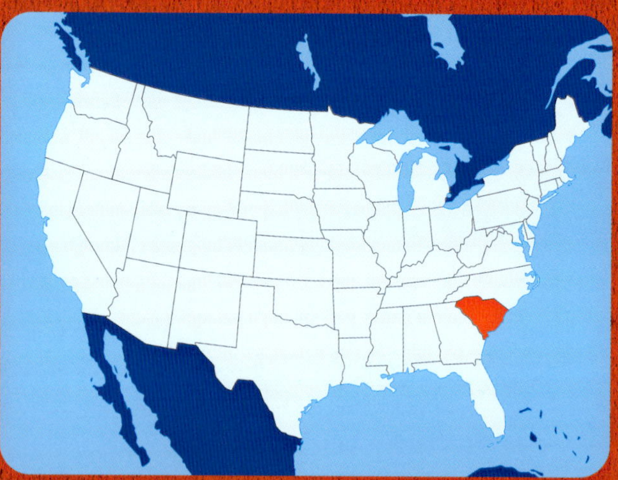

Arthur Ravenel Jr. Bridge

Darlington Raceway

Charleston

South Carolina: The Palmetto State

Glossary

annual
happening every year

cargo
goods that are moved on a vehicle, such as a ship

enslaved
forced to work without being paid

plantations
farms that are worked by people who live on the property

port
a place where ships load and unload goods

settlers
people who moved to a new area

stays
strong ropes that hold up a tower

Online Resources

To learn more about South Carolina, visit our free resource websites below.

Visit **abdocorelibrary.com** or scan this QR code for free Common Core resources for teachers and students, including vetted activities, multimedia, and booklinks, for deeper subject comprehension.

Visit **abdobooklinks.com** or scan this QR code for free additional online weblinks for further learning. These links are routinely monitored and updated to provide the most current information available.

Learn More

Cooper, Robert. *Clemson Tigers.* Abdo, 2021.

Tekiela, Stan. *Kids' Guide to Birds of the Carolinas.* Adventure, 2022.

Tieck, Sarah. *South Carolina.* Abdo, 2020.

Index

About the Author

David J. Clarke is a freelance writer. Originally from Helena, Montana, he now lives in Savannah, Georgia, with his golden retriever, Gus.